HANNAH ELEMENTARY SCH LIBY

P9-CDM-415

WITHDRAWN

Put Beginning Readers on the Right Track with ALL ABOARD READING™

The All Aboard Reading series is especially for beginning readers. Written by noted authors and illustrated in full color, these are books that children really and truly *want* to read—books to excite their imagination, tickle their funny bone, expand their interests, and support their feelings. With four different reading levels, All Aboard Reading lets you choose which books are most appropriate for your children and their growing abilities.

Picture Readers—for Ages 3 to 6
Picture Readers have super-simple texts, with many nouns appearing as rebus pictures. At the end of each book are 24 flash cards—on one side is the rebus picture; on the other side is the written-out word.

Level 1—for Preschool through First-Grade Children
Level 1 books have very few lines per page, very large type, easy words, lots of repetition, and pictures with visual "cues" to help children figure out the words on the page.

Level 2—for First-Grade to Third-Grade Children
Level 2 books are printed in slightly smaller type than Level 1 books. The stories are more complex, but there is still lots of repetition in the text, and many pictures. The sentences are quite simple and are broken up into short lines to make reading easier.

Level 3—for Second-Grade through Third-Grade Children
Level 3 books have considerably longer texts, harder words, and more complicated sentences.

All Aboard for happy reading!

To Bill, for all your help and support.
Special thanks to Bat Conservation International
and Paul Dyer Photography — Judith Moffatt

Thanks to Pat Thomas, Mammal Department, International Wildlife Conservation Park (Bronx Zoo).

Copyright © 1993 by Joyce Milton. Illustrations copyright © 1993 by Judith Moffatt. All rights reserved. Published by Grosset & Dunlap, Inc., a member of Penguin Putnam Books for Young Readers, New York. ALL ABOARD READING is a trademark of The Putnam & Grosset Group. GROSSET & DUNLAP is a trademark of Grosset & Dunlap, Inc. Published simultaneously in Canada. Printed in the U.S.A.

Library of Congress Cataloging-in-Publication Data

Milton, Joyce.
Bats : creatures of the night / by Joyce Milton ; illustrated by Judith Moffatt.
p. cm. — (All aboard reading.)
Summary: Describes the physical characteristics, behavior, and habitats of different kinds of bats.
1. Bats—Juvenile literature. [1. Bats.] I. Moffatt, Judith, ill. II. Title. III. Series.
QL737.C5M67 1993
599.4—dc20 92-43198

ISBN 0-448-40193-2 H I J

ALL ABOARD READING™

Level 2
Grades 1–3

BATS

CREATURES OF THE NIGHT

By Joyce Milton
Illustrated by Judith Moffatt

Grosset & Dunlap • New York

No one has lived
on this farm for years.
The barn looks empty.
But it isn't!
Strange creatures are sleeping
in the loft.
As the sun goes down,
they take to the air.

They come flying out
of the windows.
They swoop low over the river.
They dart under an old bridge.

From far away
the creatures look like birds.
But who ever heard
of a bird with fur?
Close up, they look like mice.
But who ever heard
of a mouse with wings?

These strange creatures are bats.

Bats are mammals.

Just like rabbits

and horses and dogs.

Just like us.

Many people think that bats are blind.

But that's not true.

Bats have eyes and they can see.

It's just that they spend

most of the time in the dark.

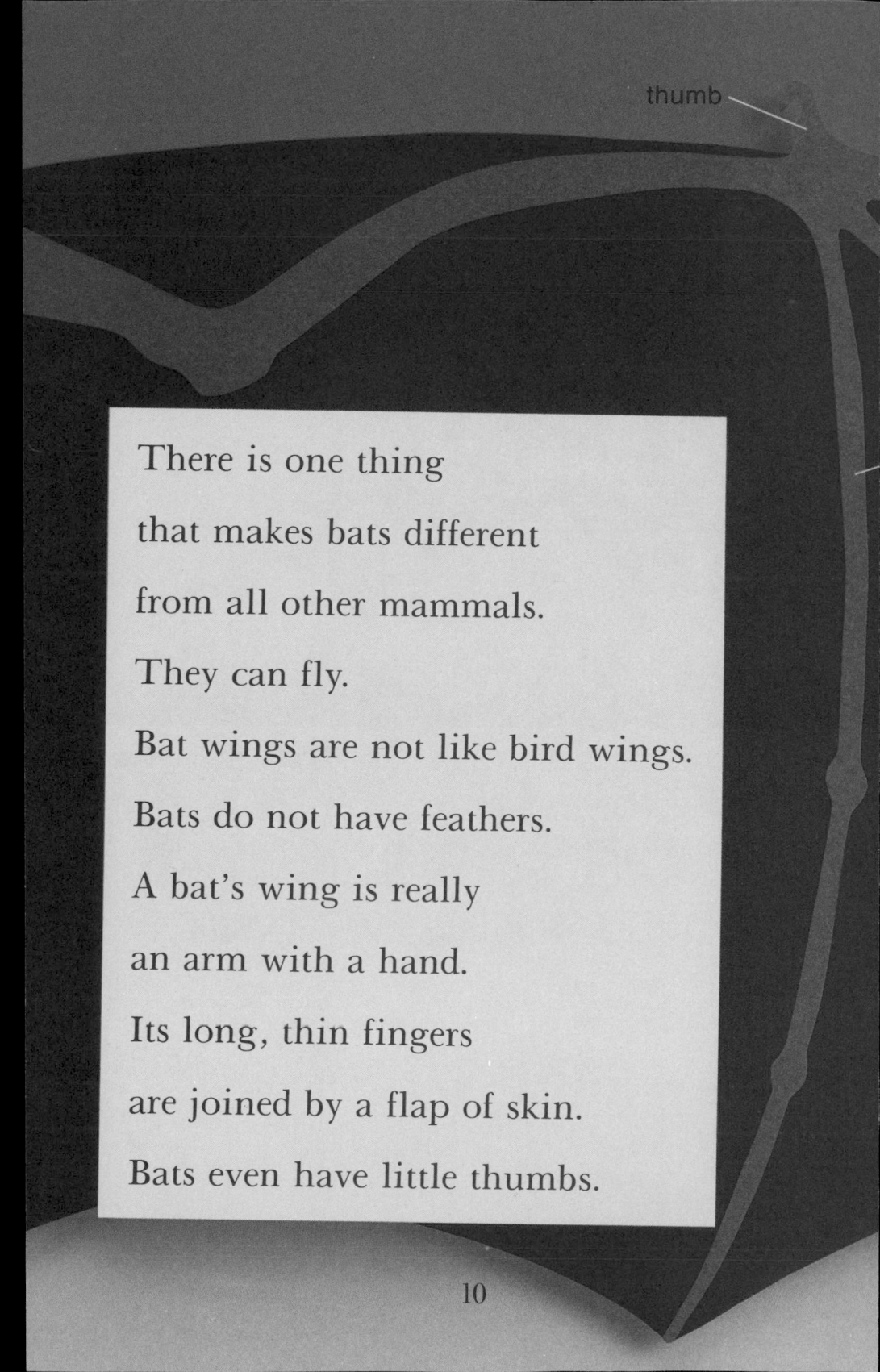

There is one thing
that makes bats different
from all other mammals.
They can fly.
Bat wings are not like bird wings.
Bats do not have feathers.
A bat's wing is really
an arm with a hand.
Its long, thin fingers
are joined by a flap of skin.
Bats even have little thumbs.

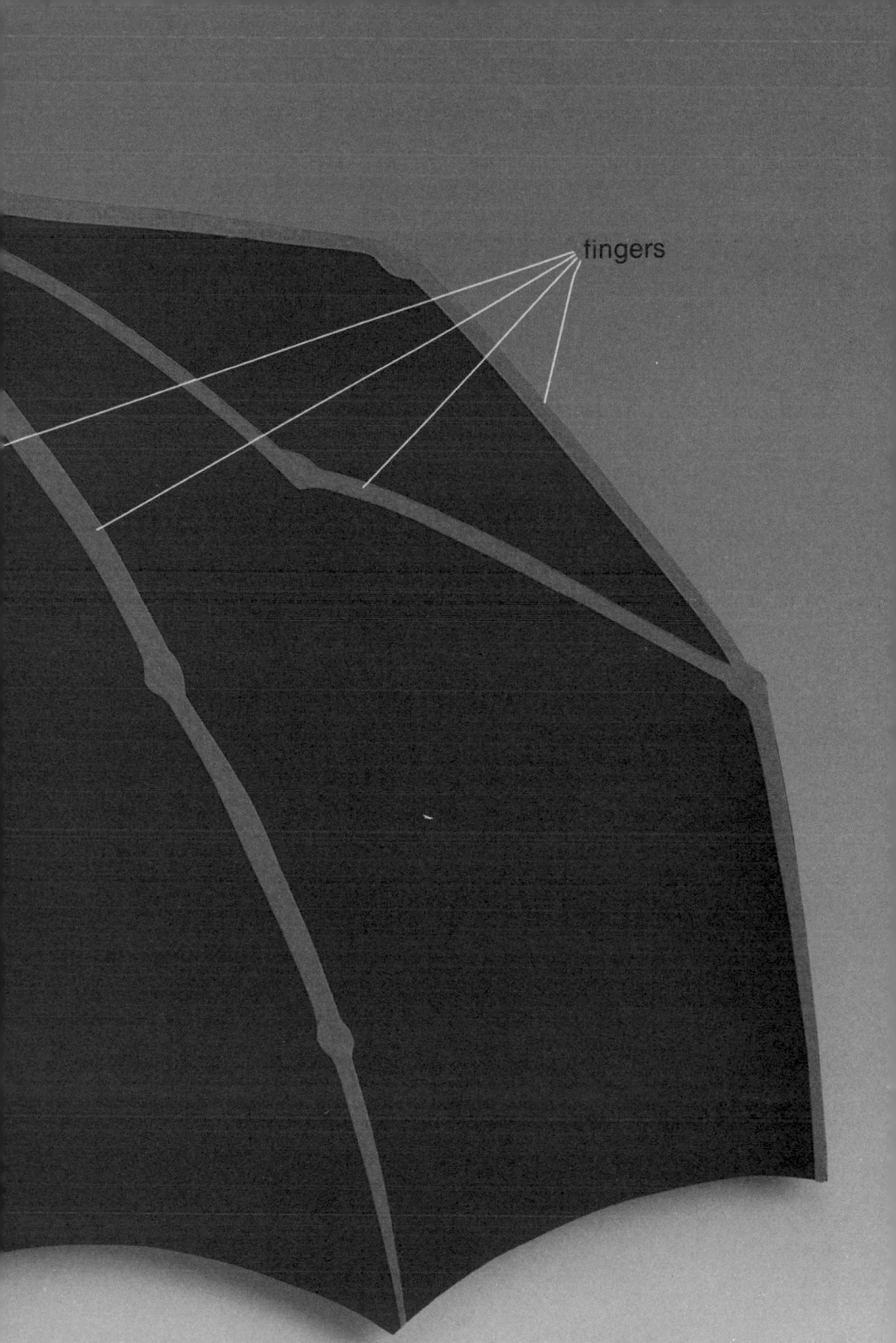
fingers

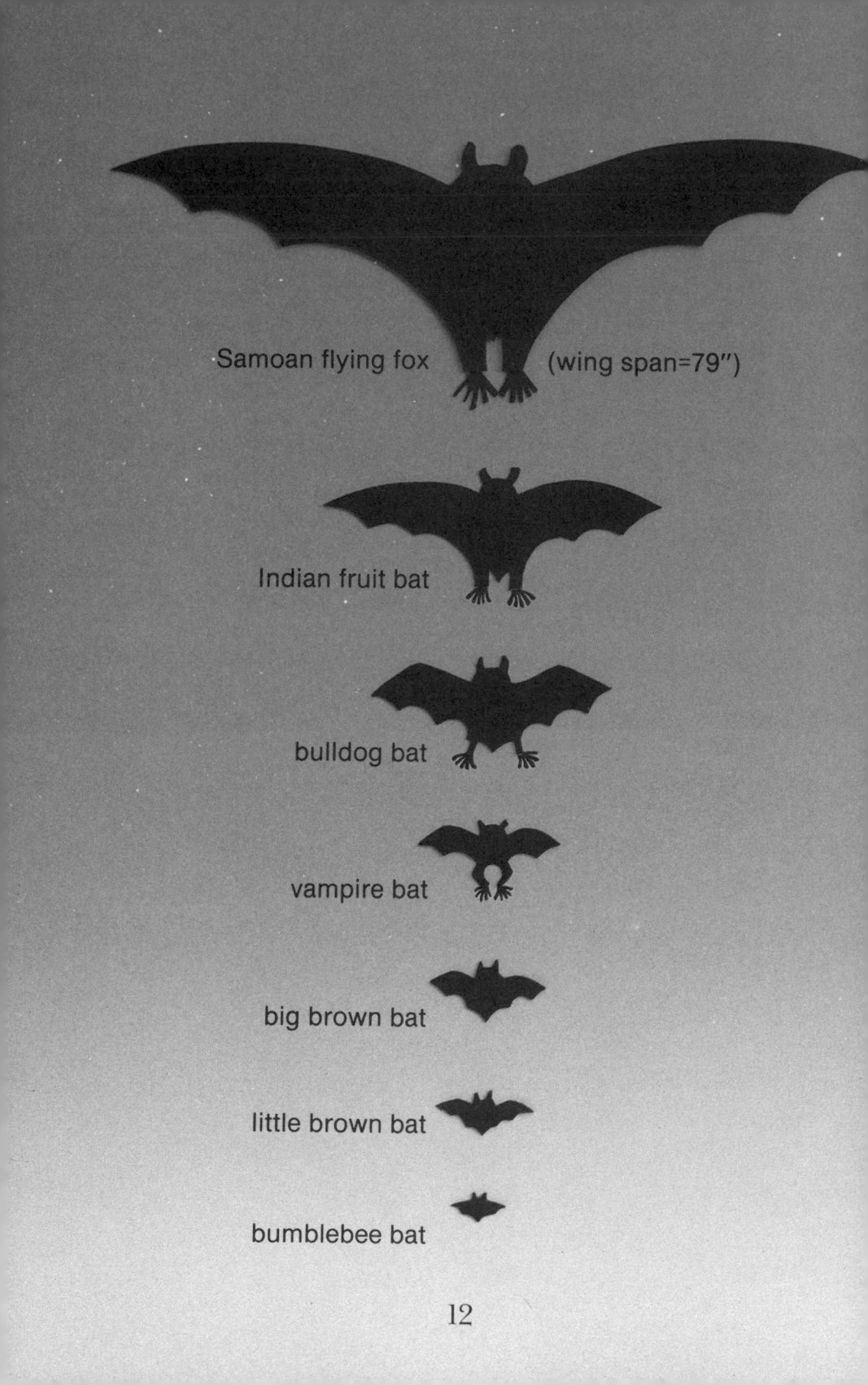
Samoan flying fox
(wing span=79″)
Indian fruit bat
bulldog bat
vampire bat
big brown bat
little brown bat
bumblebee bat

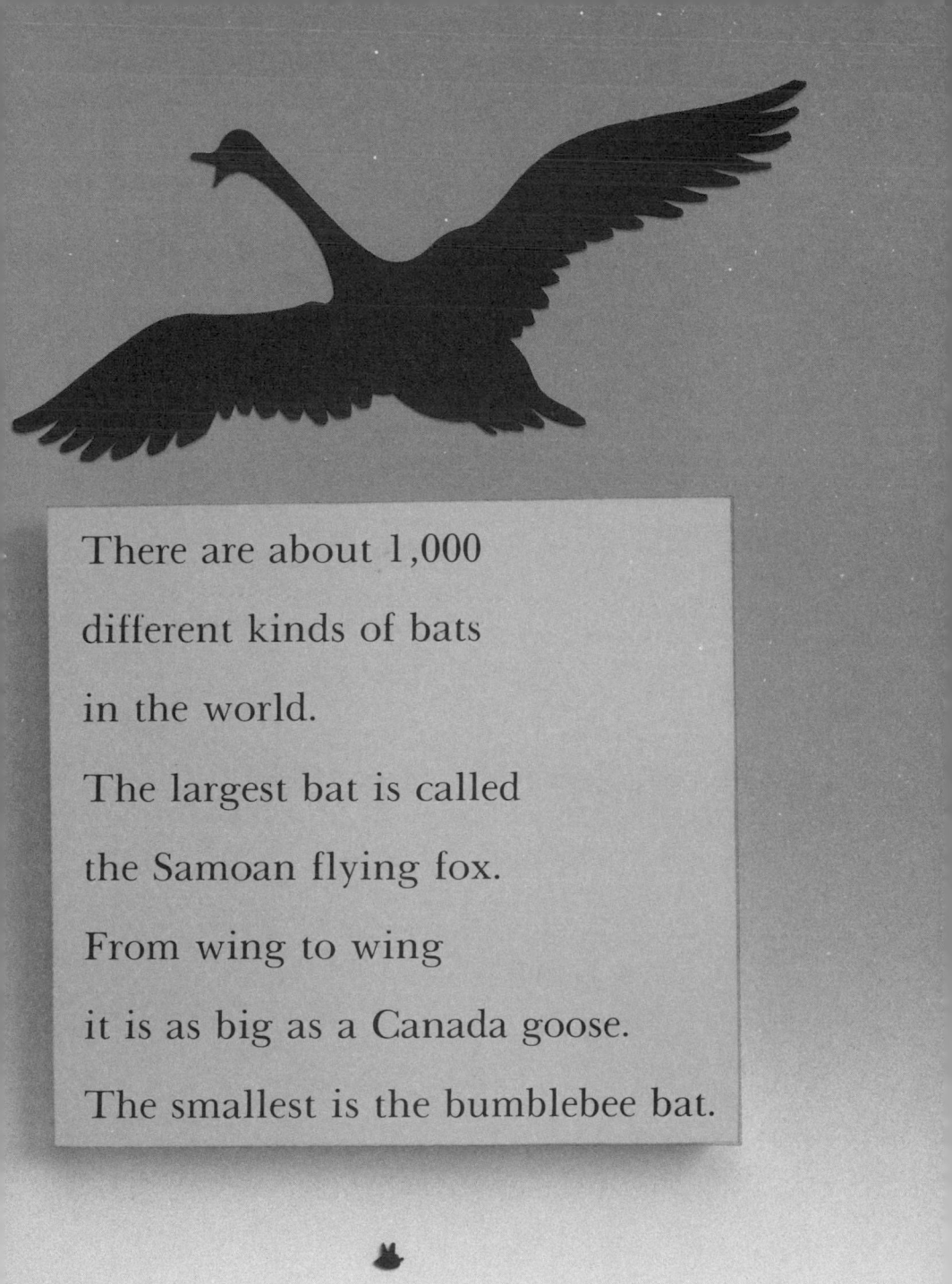

There are about 1,000
different kinds of bats
in the world.
The largest bat is called
the Samoan flying fox.
From wing to wing
it is as big as a Canada goose.
The smallest is the bumblebee bat.

You have probably heard
of the vampire bat.
Does the vampire bat
really drink the blood of animals?
Yes, it does.
It lives in Mexico and South America
where it bites cows and horses.
Are vampire bats dangerous to people?

No.

Like other bats, they are less dangerous

than raccoons, skunks, and

other wild creatures.

What do other bats like to eat?

Some eat fruit.

Some drink the juices of flowers,

just as hummingbirds do.

The bulldog bat even catches fish!

But most bats eat insects—

flies, moths, and mosquitoes.

This spotted bat
is about to catch a moth.
How can it find insects
in the dark?
It uses its ears!
A bat makes noises
when it flies—
click, click, click!

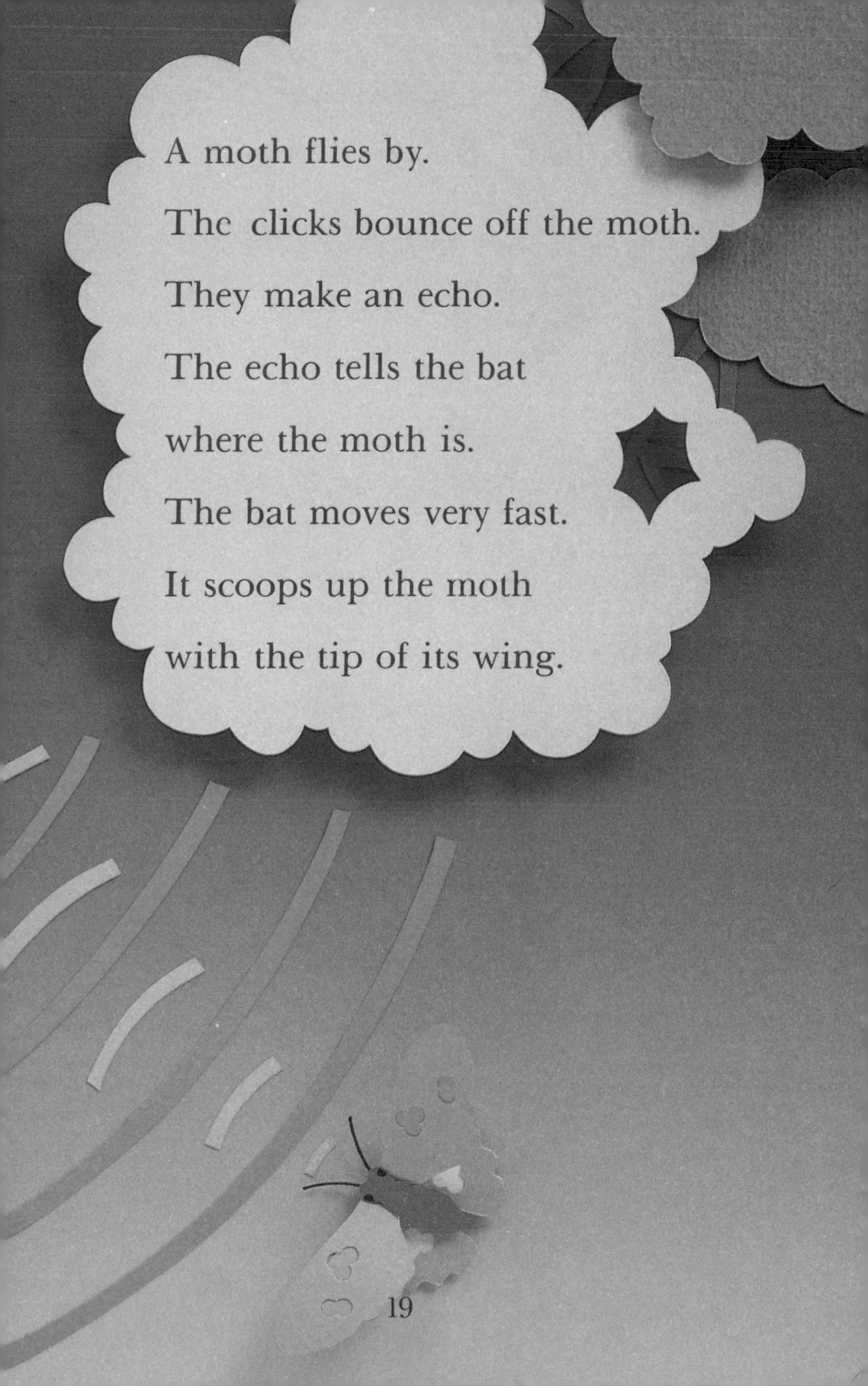

A moth flies by.
The clicks bounce off the moth.
They make an echo.
The echo tells the bat
where the moth is.
The bat moves very fast.
It scoops up the moth
with the tip of its wing.

Bats hunt only at night.

During the day they sleep.

This old barn is home to about

100 little brown bats.

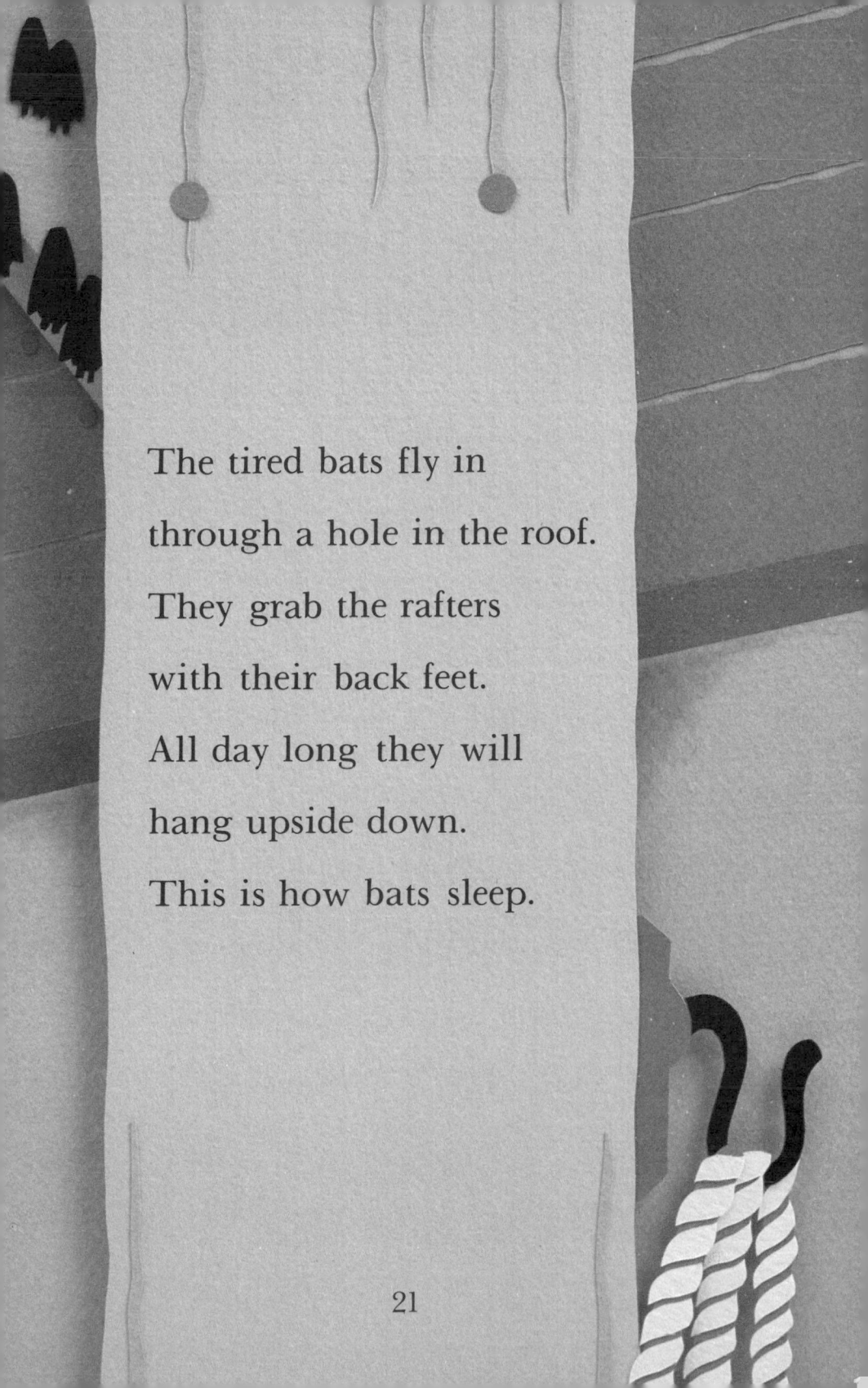

The tired bats fly in
through a hole in the roof.
They grab the rafters
with their back feet.
All day long they will
hang upside down.
This is how bats sleep.

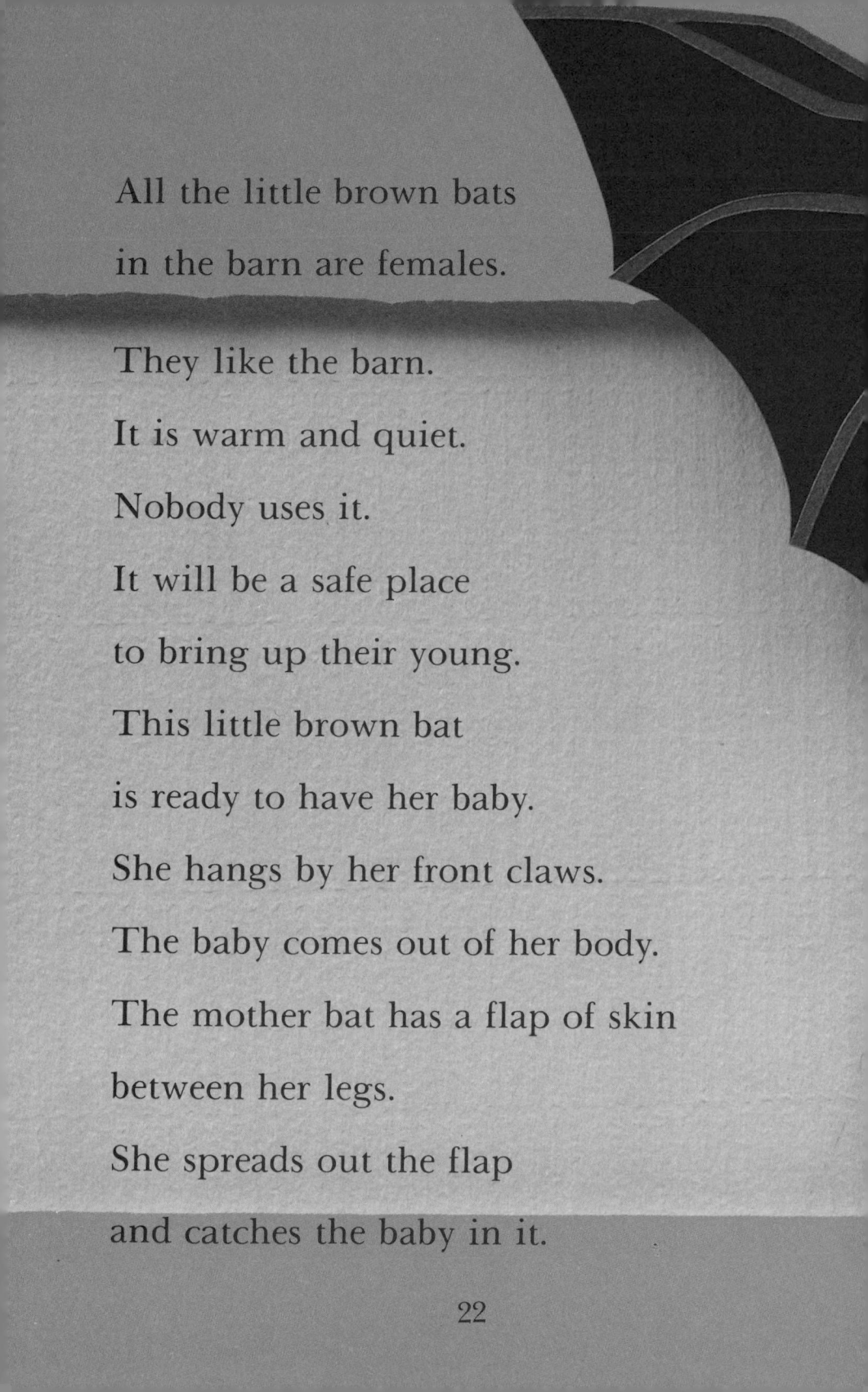

All the little brown bats
in the barn are females.

They like the barn.
It is warm and quiet.
Nobody uses it.
It will be a safe place
to bring up their young.
This little brown bat
is ready to have her baby.
She hangs by her front claws.
The baby comes out of her body.
The mother bat has a flap of skin
between her legs.
She spreads out the flap
and catches the baby in it.

The mother has to move fast!

It is a long way

to the floor of the barn.

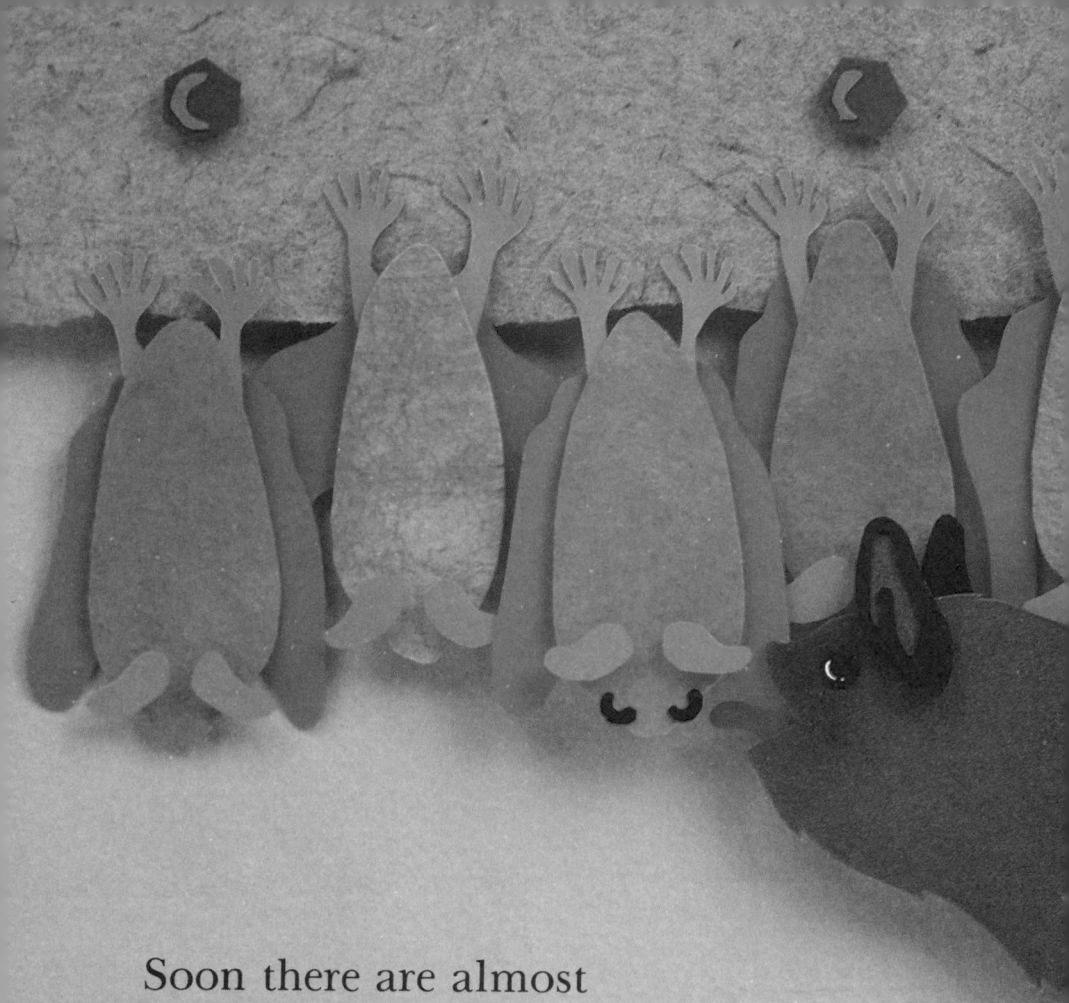

Soon there are almost
100 baby bats in the old barn.
At night, the mother bats
go out to hunt.
When they come back,
all the babies are crying for food—
wheek, wheek, wheek!

Each mother knows her own baby's voice.

She flies right to it.

She washes its face

and lets it drink some of her milk.

By the end of August,
the nights are getting colder.
The mother cannot find enough
insects to eat.
It is time for the little brown bats
to move to a different home
for the winter.

Night after night they fly.
One morning, just before sunrise,
they come to a big cave.

Male and female bats
will sleep in the cave all winter.
Thousands of bats
come back to the same cave
every year.

When spring comes,
the bats wake up slowly.
They squeak and fly
around the cave.
Then one evening, all the bats
fly out the door of the cave.
Whoosh!

Outside the cave,
a barn owl
sits high in a tree.
Suddenly the owl swoops down!
Just in time, the young bat
darts out of the way.

The little brown bat
may live to be 20 years old.
During the summers
he will not live with his mother.

He will join a group of male bats under an old bridge.

Little brown bats usually live
in the country.
Another kind of bat,
the big brown bat,
is often seen in cities.
Sometimes it sleeps
in church steeples
or in attics.

A big brown bat may even fly right through an open window.

Big brown bats are
peaceful animals.
If one gets into your house,
don't be scared.
It is probably a young bat.
It is probably lost
and scared, too.

Why are so many people
afraid of bats?
Maybe they have heard that bats
like to land in people's hair.
But that's not true!

Some people even believe
stories about vampires—
like Count Dracula.
Dracula could turn into a bat.
He drank the blood
of sleeping people.
But Dracula is not a real person.
You will only meet him in books
and horror movies.

In China people are not afraid of bats.
They think that seeing a bat is good luck.
A good gift is a lucky charm
with a picture of five flying bats.
It is a sign of happiness.

Years ago there were many more bats.
Some caves had millions of them.
Now many of those caves
have been filled in.
Some have been turned into tunnels
for cars.

Hikers sometimes disturb bats, too.
If bats wake up
in the middle of winter,
they can starve to death.
This is because there are no
insects to eat!

Now scientists are starting
to protect bat caves.
Some people are even building
bat houses.
Bats can live in them
during the summer.

Bats help to control insects.
A tiny bat can catch
up to 600 mosquitoes in an hour.
One thing bats do not like is pollution.
If there are lots of bats around,
it means the air and water
are probably clean.

That's why it really is good luck

to see a bat!